Neil Armstrong

History Maker Bios

Shannon Zemlicka

BARNES & NOBLE

NEW YORK

For Scott Barefield, my big brother and favorite pilot

The quotes in this book have been drawn from many sources,
and are assumed to be accurate as quoted in their previously published forms.
Although every effort has been made to verify the quote and sources,
the publishers cannot guarantee their perfect accuracy.

All Web sites and URLs in this book are current at the point of publication.
However, Web sites may be taken down and URLs may change after publication
without notice. The Publisher and the Author are not responsible for the content
contained in any specific Web site featured in this book, nor shall they be liable
for any loss or damage arising from the information contained in this book.

Illustrations by Tim Parlin

ISBN-13: 978-0-7607-3392-9
ISBN-10: 0-7607-3392-9

Printed and bound in China

7 9 10 8 6

TABLE OF CONTENTS

INTRODUCTION

Neil Armstrong was the first person to walk on the Moon. All his life, he wanted to fly. As a teenager, he earned his pilot's license before his driver's license.

When Neil grew up, he found a wonderful job testing new kinds of planes. Then, in 1962, he was chosen to become an astronaut and fly into space. Back then, the Moon was a mysterious place. People had dreamed of reaching it for hundreds of years. But no one had ever tried to land a spacecraft there. In 1969, Neil led a crew safely to the Moon and back. His skill and bravery helped make a great American dream come true.

This is his story.

1 FLY BOY

One calm Sunday in 1936, a six-year-old boy's life changed forever. The boy's name was Neil Armstrong. He was supposed to be at church. Instead, his father had taken him for his first airplane ride.

The plane was a small, metal craft called a Tin Goose. Neil gazed down through its windows at farmhouses and cars. He listened to the whir of the propellers and the hum of the motors. He felt the plane glide and bounce on bumpy air currents.

From that day on, Neil wanted to fly and fly and fly.

Not many people flew in airplanes during the 1930s. Flying was expensive, and many Americans had a hard time just paying their bills and keeping their families fed. The Armstrongs were better off than many people. Neil's father, Stephen, had a good job. He worked for the government of Ohio.

Neil's first airplane ride was in a Ford Trimotor, also known as a Tin Goose.

Like many children in the 1930s, Neil did his part to help his family by getting a job. He gave most of the money he earned to his parents, but he got to keep some for himself. His first job was cutting grass in a graveyard. It paid ten cents an hour—just enough for a model airplane kit. By the time he was nine, Neil was decorating his bedroom with planes hung from the ceiling.

THE GREAT DEPRESSION

Neil grew up during a difficult time in the United States called the Great Depression. From 1929 to the early 1940s, many Americans could not find work. Thousands of people lost their homes. Some had to live in cars or in shacks made of packing crates. Neil's family had a comfortable life compared to some. But like everyone, they used what they had carefully. Neil powered his model planes with rubber bands, not expensive engines.

Young Neil in his band uniform

When Neil wasn't working or building model planes, he was usually reading. Sometimes he liked reading about airplanes better than playing with other kids. He especially enjoyed the story of the Wright brothers, who invented the first plane in 1903.

Neil grew into a quiet, shy young man. He wasn't much good at sports, but he loved music.

Neil was thirteen when the Armstrongs moved to the small town of Wapakoneta, Ohio. A neighbor there, Jacob Zint, had a telescope. He let Neil and the other neighborhood kids look through it. Most would peek at the stars and the Moon for a minute or two. But Neil couldn't seem to stop staring.

Two years later, Neil got himself back into an airplane at last. He started taking flying lessons at an airport near Wapakoneta. After enough lessons, he would be able to take a test to earn his pilot's license.

The Armstrong house in Wapakoneta, Ohio

In high school, Neil played the baritone horn in a jazz band called The Mississippi Moonshiners.

Each lesson cost nine dollars an hour. Neil worked at a drugstore, a hardware store, and a bakery to pay his way. It took him more than twenty hours of work to earn the money for one lesson, but soaring through the sky was worth it.

On his sixteenth birthday, Neil received the best possible present—his pilot's license. Now he could fly on his own! He had to hitch a ride home from the airport to tell his parents the good news. Although he could fly a plane, he didn't have a driver's license yet.

It was time to plan for the future. Neil wanted to learn to design and build new kinds of airplanes. But his parents couldn't afford to pay for college.

Once again, Neil worked hard to meet his goal. He studied hard, worked his odd jobs, and flew whenever he could.

In 1946, Neil won a scholarship to Purdue University in Indiana. The United States Navy would pay for his education. In return, he would join the navy for a while after college. That sounded good to Neil—the navy had plenty of pilots. At age seventeen, he was on his way to a future in the sky.

2 EARNING HIS WINGS

Neil started college in 1947. After just a year and a half, he had to leave college and join the navy. The United States was about to go to war in Asia. They needed pilots.

Neil was a bit nervous. What if he crashed? What if he made a mistake that hurt his copilot? He decided to train on a one-person plane. That way, if he made mistakes he would hurt only himself.

Soon, though, Neil got used to flying under pressure. In 1951 and 1952, he flew seventy-eight missions, bombing enemy tanks and bridges. His work in the Korean War earned him three medals. He became known as a pilot who could handle all kinds of danger.

Neil was only nineteen years old when he joined the navy to fight in the Korean War.

In the war, Neil flew Panther jets, which took off from huge ships called aircraft carriers.

One of his most dangerous missions almost cost him his life. Neil collided with a cable, a trap set by the enemy to damage planes. His plane lost the tip of a wing. Neil coaxed the injured craft back to safe territory. Then he parachuted to the ground, landing safely in a rice field.

Neil went back to college after serving in the war. To earn money, he delivered newspapers before most students were even awake. As Neil trooped across campus, he met another early riser on her way to class. Her name was Janet Shearon.

Janet's father owned a small plane, so she knew a lot about flying. She also shared Neil's love of music. Neil liked her, but he wasn't a person to rush things. It took him two years to ask her for a date.

Neil finished college in 1955. He headed to the best place for eager young pilots, Edwards Air Force Base in California. There the American government was building and testing new kinds of airplanes—just what Neil wanted to do.

Neil and Janet were married in January 1956.

In the X-15 rocket plane, Neil zoomed at speeds of up to four thousand miles per hour, forty miles above the ground.

He didn't leave Janet behind for long. They married in 1956, when Neil was twenty-five. Their first child, Eric, was born in 1957. Then a daughter, Karen, came along in 1959.

Neil loved his young family and his work. His most exciting job was testing the X-15 rocket plane. In it, he flew almost forty miles high. That far above Earth, he didn't see farmhouses and cars when he looked down. He saw a round planet.

Flying the X-15 was almost as good as going into space. Neil hoped that one day a rocket plane would take him all the way there. But in the summer of 1961, he suddenly had more than space travel on his mind. Little Karen became very ill. She died in January 1962.

While Neil grieved for his daughter, John Glenn became the first American to circle Earth from space. This remarkable achievement, called orbiting, didn't happen in a rocket plane. Glenn traveled in a cone-shaped capsule powered by a rocket.

Astronaut John Glenn shows President John F. Kennedy (who is looking in the window) the space capsule in which he orbited Earth.

SPACE RACE

Exploring space was not just about astronauts and rockets. In the 1960s, it was a contest between two countries. The Soviet Union sent the first person into space in April 1961. The United States didn't want to be left behind. That year, President John F. Kennedy set an important goal. He vowed that by the end of the 1960s, America would put a person on the Moon.

Neil knew he would have to become an astronaut like John Glenn to get to space. He applied to America's space program at NASA, the National Aeronautics and Space Administration. Out of hundreds of hopeful pilots, Neil and eight others were chosen in September 1962.

The Armstrongs headed for Houston. This hot, sunny city in Texas was where astronauts were trained. Neil hoped it would be a good place to call home.

3 SPACE EXPLORER

Houston did become a good home for the Armstrongs. As Neil settled into his new job, he and Janet prepared to welcome a new child. Mark was born in 1963.

Neil had a lot to learn about being an astronaut. In space, people and objects float unless they are anchored down. Neil trained in a special room that imitated this strange environment. He also learned to fly a space capsule in a model called a simulator. He tried on space suits and studied ways to deal with emergencies.

Neil didn't mind working so hard. Doing a job well was a person's best chance to be happy, he thought. His effort paid off. After years of training, he was named commander of a mission called *Gemini 8.* He was going to space at last.

Neil in his space suit

Neil and David Scott just before boarding GEMINI 8

The goal of *Gemini 8* was to join two vehicles together in space. No one had ever docked space vehicles before. The task would be a challenge for Neil and his copilot, David Scott. If the mission succeeded, docking would be an important part of NASA's plan to reach the Moon.

On March 16, 1966, the thirty-five-year-old astronaut climbed into a space capsule. This time, it was a real one, not a simulator. The last seconds of the countdown ticked away. Three . . . Two . . . One . . . Liftoff!

A huge rocket roared
into the sky with Neil and
David's capsule attached.
As *Gemini 8* zoomed
higher, Neil looked down
at Earth. He spotted the
islands of Hawaii in the
Pacific Ocean. Then the
sun set, and darkness
spread around the capsule.
Neil could see fire
streaming from the
capsule's thrusters as they
powered the craft along.

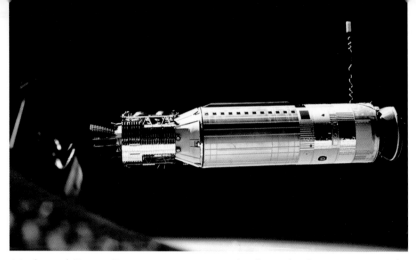

Neil and David's mission was to dock with this unmanned rocket.

The astronauts flew twice around Earth. Then they spotted their target. It was an unmanned rocket that had becn launched into space ahead of *Gemini 8*. Neil and David carefully guided their capsule toward the rocket. They lined the vehicles up and docked them together. Success!

Then something went wrong. The capsule and rocket began to spin out of control. Neil undocked the capsule from the rocket. To his horror, the spinning grew faster. The astronauts felt dizzy. If the spinning kept up, they would eventually pass out. And if they passed out, the violent spinning would kill them.

Neil and David stayed calm. Neil hit the capsule's thrusters, timing the thrusts to even out the spinning. It worked! *Gemini 8* slowed enough for the astronauts to regain control. Later, the astronauts learned that one of the capsule's thrusters had gotten stuck in the "on" position. The extra thrusting had caused the spinning.

Since the capsule was unsafe to fly, the mission had to end. Neil and David guided *Gemini 8* to an emergency splashdown in the Pacific Ocean. The men were rescued and brought home.

When Neil and David landed in the ocean, a yellow raft inflated around their capsule to help it float. Green dye came out of the front to help rescuers find the men.

Neil's first trip into space had almost killed him. But at least he and David had proved that spacecraft could be docked.

In January 1969, Neil learned that his next mission would have a much more difficult goal. NASA named him commander of *Apollo 11.* For the first time, human beings would try to land on the Moon. Neil Armstrong would be their leader.

SPACE FOOD

In some ways, life in space was like life on Earth. The astronauts had to sleep and go to the bathroom. They also had to eat. For supper, Neil and David added water to packets of dried chicken casserole. When they had to tend to the capsule's controls, they just let the casseroles float up to the ceiling.

4 MAN ON THE MOON

For six months, Neil trained harder than he ever had. He practiced for many hours flying a vehicle like the one he would land on the Moon. To find out how it would feel to walk in the Moon's low gravity, he strapped on weights and trudged around in a huge water tank.

Neil was also fitted for new space suits and taught about the Moon's surface. He even learned how to survive in the jungle in case he had to make an emergency landing in a jungle on Earth.

Janet worried that he seemed pale and tense. Neil had good reasons to be tense. Many things could go wrong in space travel. In 1967, three astronauts had died in a fire while training for *Apollo 1*. No one knew for certain that landing on the Moon would be safe. And if anything kept Neil from taking off from the Moon when it was time to leave, there would be no way to rescue him.

Neil practices climbing down a ladder like the one he would later use on the Moon.

The crew of
APOLLO 11.
LEFT TO RIGHT:
Neil, Michael
Collins, and
Buzz Aldrin

Neil trained so quietly and intensely that some of the other astronauts thought he was unfriendly. As they got to know him, they realized that he was simply keeping his eyes on the goal. Besides, he was still a bit shy, just as he had been as a boy.

Finally the long hours of training were over. On July 16, 1969, the crew of *Apollo 11* entered their capsule. Neil was joined by two other astronauts, Buzz Aldrin and Michael Collins. He also brought along two symbols of success in the air—pieces of the wing and propeller from the Wright brothers' first airplane.

Millions of people watched on television as a huge rocket shot into space, carrying the astronauts in their capsule. They were on their way.

After three days of flight, the Moon came into view. Neil thought it looked magnificent—both beautiful and friendly.

The next day, *Apollo 11* split into two spacecraft. Michael Collins stayed behind in *Columbia.* He would orbit the Moon while Neil and Buzz headed down to the surface in *Eagle.*

Neil's wife, Janet, and their two sons, Eric (LEFT) and Mark (RIGHT). The family talked to reporters after APOLLO 11 had blasted off and was heading for the Moon.

Columbia flying over the Moon. This photo was taken after *Eagle* and *Columbia* had separated.

The skinny legs of *Eagle* were specially built to land on the Moon and take off again. It would rejoin *Columbia* later in order to return to Earth.

"The *Eagle* has wings," Neil radioed to Earth as the two spacecraft separated.

At first, *Eagle* flew on automatic pilot toward the Moon. Through the windows, Neil and Buzz saw a problem. The planned landing area was cluttered with rocks the size of cars. *Eagle* could not land safely here.

Neil took over the controls. Fuel was running out. If he didn't land soon, he would have to give up and return to *Columbia.*

With just forty seconds of fuel left, Neil spotted a flat, clear patch of ground. Slowly, he eased *Eagle* down. The landing was so gentle that the astronauts barely felt it. Neil and Buzz shook hands. They were on the Moon!

Neil inside EAGLE as it sat on the Moon. After arriving safely, he radioed back to Earth, "The EAGLE has landed."

Until July 20, 1969, no human being had ever made a footprint on the Moon.

The astronauts got their equipment ready. They put on heavy space suits, helmets, gloves, and boots. The world would be watching on television when Neil stepped onto the Moon's surface. What would he say? He had been asking himself that question for weeks. His words would have to capture the thrill of the moment for the many people all over the world who shared his dream.

Neil climbed down *Eagle*'s ladder. Many years ago, he had gazed at the Moon through Jacob Zint's telescope. Now he was about to walk on it.

Carefully, he stepped down. Television cameras on *Eagle* recorded every movement and beamed the images back to Earth. Radio signals carried the sounds. The world waited to hear what Neil's first words would be.

"That's one small step for man, one giant leap for mankind."

The Moon was as beautiful as Neil had imagined. The sky above was dark, but the sun's rays lit the surface with a warm glow. Rocks of all shapes and sizes dotted the surface. Fine, powdery dust covered the ground.

THE MISSING "A"

Neil actually meant his first words on the Moon to be, "That's one small step for a man, one giant leap for mankind." But no one on Earth heard the "a" before "man." It may have been lost in the radio transmission. Or Neil may have been so excited that he forgot to say it at all.

The flag Neil and Buzz planted had wires in it to make it stiff, so it looked like it was waving. There is no air or wind on the Moon, so a flag without wires would have hung limp instead of waving.

Neil could see Earth, too: blue oceans, brown land, swirling white clouds. It looked much larger than the Moon looks from Earth.

A few minutes later, Buzz followed Neil down the ladder. The astronauts went to work. They collected samples of rocks and soil for scientists to study. They planted an American flag. They took pictures and received a phone call from President Richard Nixon.

Neil wished he had more time. There was so much to explore! But the astronauts only had enough air for about two and a half hours. Soon they had to return to *Eagle*.

Neil and Buzz spent the night safely inside the spacecraft. Then Neil fired up the engine. Back on Earth, Janet and the boys waited nervously. Would *Eagle* be up to its final test? It was. With a rush of flame, it blasted off from the Moon.

Neil took this famous photo of Buzz on the Moon. You can see the reflections of Neil and Eagle in Buzz's mask.

Eagle flies up to dock with *Columbia*. Half of Earth is visible above the surface of the Moon.

The American astronauts left behind their flag, their footprints, and a plaque. Along with their signatures, it carried a message for future visitors: "We came in peace for all mankind."

After a few hours of flight, *Eagle* docked with *Columbia*. On the way home, Neil radioed Earth with a message of thanks to the American scientists whose work had made the trip possible.

Three days later, the crew splashed down safely in the Pacific Ocean. *Apollo 11* had made exploration history. And the men on the Moon had made it home to Earth.

5 BACK ON EARTH

Neil and his crew couldn't go straight home after their splashdown. The American government was worried. Had the crew brought back dangerous germs from the Moon? For safety, the astronauts spent two weeks in a sealed room on the ship that picked them up from the ocean. Fortunately, no Moon germs made the astronauts sick.

After they landed back on Earth, the astronauts spent two weeks in this sealed room. They had some visitors, including President Richard Nixon.

When the men were set free at last, Neil joked that he would *pretend* to be sick if anyone pointed a camera at him. He had to face much more than a few cameras, though. The whole world wanted to meet the men who had gone to the Moon.

The *Apollo 11* crew reunited with their families, rode in parades, and had dinner with President Nixon. They spent more than a month traveling through twenty-five countries across the world. Neil met the queen of England and the emperor of Japan.

Neil's tour took him to Vietnam to greet soldiers who were fighting there.

After the tour, he hoped that life would get back to normal. But there was no such thing as normal for him anymore. Everywhere he went, people recognized him. Fans begged for his autograph and his picture. Neil missed the quiet, private life that he and Janet had built.

In 1971, Neil made a change. He took a teaching job at the University of Cincinnati in Ohio. The Armstrongs bought a dairy farm outside the city.

The new job wasn't perfect. At first, excited students stood on each other's shoulders to peer into Neil's office window. Over time, people got used to seeing him on campus.

Neil liked farming. Milking cows and working in the dirt reminded him that he was just one of many living things on Earth. That was how he had always seen himself, and that was how he liked it.

In 1980, Neil left the university. Six years later, a terrible disaster brought him close to NASA once again. On January 28, 1986, the space shuttle *Challenger* launched. Seconds after the launch, the shuttle suddenly exploded. The entire crew was killed.

A BIGGER STEP

NASA's next mission to the Moon was *Apollo 12* in November 1969. Astronaut Pete Conrad became the third person to walk on the Moon. Conrad was five feet, six inches tall—rather short for an astronaut. When he hopped down to the Moon's surface, he exclaimed, "Man, that may have been a small one for Neil, but that's a long one for me."

The space shuttle
CHALLENGER exploded
shortly after it took
off. One of the seven
crew members was
Christa McAuliffe,
who would have been
the first teacher in
space.

Neil shared the nation's shock and grief for the lost space explorers. How could another accident be prevented? Neil worked with scientists to investigate what went wrong. They discovered that a mechanical problem had caused the accident, and the problem was fixed on other space shuttles.

The first man to walk on the Moon still lives a quiet life in Ohio. He spends time with his grandchildren, reads, and enjoys music. He also keeps his distance from fans and reporters. In this way, he has regained some of the privacy he lost after *Apollo 11.*

Of course, people still ask Neil Armstrong about that famous trip. He is as proud as ever to have gone. But to him, the credit belongs to many. Hundreds of people at NASA worked for years to send astronauts to the Moon. To Neil, those people are as important as the astronauts themselves.

Besides, walking on the Moon wasn't nearly as much fun as getting there was. "Pilots take no special joy in walking," he explained once. "Pilots like flying."

On July 20, 1999, Neil (CENTER), Michael (LEFT), and Buzz (RIGHT) celebrated the thirtieth anniversary of their trip to the Moon.

TIMELINE

In the year . . .

1936   Neil rode in a Tin Goose airplane with his dad.   `Age 6`

1946   he earned his pilot's license on August 5, his sixteenth birthday.

1947   he started college at Purdue University in Indiana.

1949   he went into the navy to fly fighter planes in Korea.

1955   he graduated from college.

he went to Edwards Air Force Base to fly new kinds of airplanes.

1956   he married Janet Shearon.

1957   his son Eric was born.

1959   his daughter Karen was born.

1962   Karen died.

he joined NASA as an astronaut.   `Age 32`

1963   his son Mark was born.

1966   he commanded the *Gemini 8* mission.

1969   *Apollo 11* blasted off for the Moon on July 16.

he stepped onto the Moon on July 20.   `Age 38`

1971   he began teaching at the University of Cincinnati.

1986   the space shuttle *Challenger* exploded on January 28.

MORE SPACE EXPLORATION

After Neil's trip to the Moon, five more *Apollo* missions successfully landed there. A total of twelve astronauts walked on the Moon. They took more than 30,000 photographs and brought 838 pounds of moon rocks back to Earth. Since 1972, people have not returned to the Moon. NASA has kept exploring space with probes, space shuttles, and other projects.

Much of this space exploration is done with powerful telescopes instead of manned space missions. In 1990, the space shuttle *Discovery* launched the Hubble Space Telescope (HST) into orbit around the Earth. The HST can photograph stars, comets, and planets millions of miles from Earth. It sends these images back to Earth for scientists to study.

NASA began building the International Space Station (ISS), pictured here, in 1998. It is in permanent orbit around Earth. Crews living on the ISS perform experiments to learn more about space, medicine, and other areas of research.

FURTHER READING

Kerrod, Robin. *The Moon.* **Minneapolis, MN: Lerner Publications Company, 2000.** Introduces Earth's closest neighbor, the Moon, and its properties, exploration, and effects on Earth.

Maze, Stephanie, and Catherine O'Neill Grace. *I Want to Be an Astronaut.* **New York: Harcourt Brace & Company, 1997.** Describes what it is like to be an astronaut and some ways to prepare for this career.

Stott, Carole, and Richard Bonson. *Moon Landing: The Race for the Moon.* **New York: DK Publishing, Inc., 1999.** An illustrated account of humans' exploration of the Moon, from our first observations to the first landing and later expeditions.

Vogt, Gregory. *Exploring Space.* **Austin, TX: Raintree Steck-Vaughn Publishers, 2001.** Describes the history of space exploration, from the invention of the first rockets to modern missions such as the Hubble Space Telescope.

WEBSITES

The Apollo Program
<www.nasm.si.edu/apollo/> This website, which is part of the National Air and Space Museum of the Smithsonian Institution, provides images and information about all the manned *Apollo* missions.

NASA
<www.nasa.gov> The website for the National Aeronautics and Space Administration provides updates on current NASA missions and detailed histories of past missions, including *Apollo 11.* It also has a "NASA for Kids" page.

SELECT BIBLIOGRAPHY

Armstrong, Neil A. "The Moon Had Been Awaiting Us a Long Time." *Life*, August 22, 1969, 24–25.

Armstrong, Neil A., Michael Collins, and Edwin E. Aldrin Jr. *First on the Moon*. Boston: Little, Brown and Company, 1970.

The First Lunar Landing: As Told by the Astronauts. N.p.: NASA, 1989.

"Gemini Astronauts." *New York Times*, March 17, 1966, L20.

Hamblin, Dora Jane. "Neil Armstrong Refuses to 'Waste Any Heartbeats.'" *Life*, July 4, 1969, 18–21.

"Men for the Moon." *Newsweek*, July 21, 1969, 72.

Purdy, Matthew. "In Rural Ohio, Armstrong Quietly Lives on His Own Dark Side of the Moon." *New York Times*, July 20, 1994, A14.

Sawyer, Kathy. "Armstrong's Code." *Washington Post*, July 11, 1999, W10.

Steven, William K. "The Crew: What Kind of Men Are They?" *New York Times*, July 17, 1969, L31.

Walsh, Patrick J. *Echoes among the Stars: A Short History of the U.S. Space Program*. Armonk, NY: M. E. Sharpe, Inc., 2000.

INDEX

Acknowledgments

For photographs: NASA, pp. 4, 17, 22, 24, 25, 28, 29, 31, 32, 33, 35, 36, 39, 42, 45; © United Airlines, p. 7; Ohio Historical Society, pp, 9, 10, 16; © Todd Strand/ Independent Picture Service, p. 11; National Archives, p. 14; © Bettmann/Corbis, pp. 15, 21, 23, 30, 40; John F. Kennedy Library, p. 18; © NASA/Corbis, p. 37; © Reuters NewMedia Inc./CORBIS, p. 43. Front and back cover, NASA.
For quoted material: pp. 31, 34, 37, Neil A. Armstrong, Michael Collins, and Edwin E. Aldrin Jr., *First on the Moon* (Boston: Little, Brown and Company, 1970); pp. 32, 41, Patrick J. Walsh, *Echoes among the Stars: A Short History of the U.S. Space Program* (Armonk, NY: M. E. Sharpe, Inc., 2000); p. 43, Kathy Sawyer, "Armstrong's Code" (*The Washington Post,* July 11, 1999, p. W10).